The

t

Developing Students' Transferable Skills

Graham Gibbs
Chris Rust
Alan Jenkins
David Jaques

© Oxford Centre for Staff Development 1994

Published by
THE OXFORD CENTRE FOR STAFF DEVELOPMENT
Oxford Brookes University
Gipsy Lane
Headington
Oxford
OX3 0BP

Developing Students' Transferable Skills ISBN 1 873576 22 6
British Library Cataloguing-in-Publication Data. A catalogue record for this book is available from the British Library.

Designed and Typeset in 10.5 on 14 pt Palatino and Helvetica by Ann Trew

Printed in Great Britain by
Oxonian Rewley Press Ltd
Oxford

Printed on paper produced from sustainable forests.

Contents

Introduction

1.1 What are transferable skills?

In the 1970s there was a growing concern about study and learning skills – the skills which had an impact on the effectiveness and outcomes of student learning. These included essay and lab report writing, using libraries, note-taking and being organised. In the 80s there was a growing awareness that study and learning skills were not only vital for effective functioning during a student's education but also had many similarities to the skills students would need in the world of work: communication skills, information skills, record keeping, and time and task management. During this period they were referred to as "transferable skills". By the late 80s this concern had been taken up by the Conservative government, and had materialised into a large programme, initiated by the Manpower Services Commission, involving some 63 institutions and £70 million in funding, to re-orientate higher education so that it more explicitly addressed the needs of industry and commerce. Initially there was fairly blatant concern for entrepreneurialism, and initiatives concentrated on links with industry, work placements and short courses in finance and management. This has evolved into a broad concern to involve students more actively in learning and to bring aspects of the world outside academia into the ways that courses are run and assessed. In particular it became widely accepted that many students were not being at all well prepared for the world of work, whether commercial or public sector. Students left higher education without being able to communicate effectively, orally or in writing, without being able to co-operate with others, computer illiterate, lacking in autonomy and unaware of the demands that jobs would make on them. Students were said to lack enterprise and initiative.

A sample list of transferable skills, that used at Oxford Brookes University (which is similar to lists used at a number of institutions), can be found in Section 2.1.

1.2 Resources for developing transferable skills: trading content for process

* Residential interns of working with others?

Developing transferable skills takes time and resources: classroom time, student time, lecturer time in preparation and marking, and sometimes some special facilities. As most institutions are under acute resource pressures and most lecturers (and students) are under severe time pressure, it is not realistic to expect transferable skills to be taken seriously unless something else is dropped from the course. Even if resources were readily available there would still have to be some tough decisions made if curricula were not to become over-full. Where transferable skills are taught separately a trade-off is easy to see. At Cheltenham and Gloucester College of Higher Education, for example, students take two compulsory skills modules in their first year. This means that they can take two fewer modules in their main subjects. It also means that large numbers of lecturers have to be involved in teaching skills to 800 or so students and they therefore cannot be used elsewhere to teach their subjects. While many well-developed transferable skills programmes are integrated into courses rather than taught separately, this does not mean that the teaching and learning of skills take no additional resources. The reality is that something has to go. It is a matter of deciding on objectives and priorities and crossing off some of those lower down the list. It usually means trading some content for some process – taking out some subject material in

Cheltenham and Gloucester College of Higher Education has two compulsory skills modules in the first year.

exchange for introducing some skills work. But changing courses to accommodate the development of transferable skills involves a good deal more than substituting one component for another.

1.3 The problem of transfer

The whole raison d'être of transferable skills is that they transfer from one situation to another – from academic contexts to work contexts and from one work context to another during increasingly unpredictable career paths. The argument runs something like this. Specific subject knowledge is becoming less valuable and what is required today is the flexibility to be effective in different situations. What these different situations have in common is not their knowledge content but their skills content and so education in preparation for these situations should focus on these common transferable skills.

All this assumes that skills transfer easily from one context to another. Some curricula have retained the academic content of their courses intact and added in a few transferable skills on the assumption that these skills will somehow transfer to contexts quite unlike the academic contexts in which they were learnt. Unfortunately things are not that simple and skills do not, in fact, transfer very readily.

Transfer of training has been a notorious and sometimes intractable problem for a whole range of generalised skills training initiatives. It can be hard to find convincing evidence that some 'transferable' skills, such as problem solving, transfer to new situations at all. Where transfer takes place its extent seems to depend largely on the similarity between the context in which the skill was learnt and the context in which the skill is subsequently used. If the contexts are very different then little benefit is experienced from the prior learning of the skill. It is a commonplace that much conventional medical education is wasted because students learn medical knowledge without learning to apply it. However, it is now also acknowledged that even in problem-based medical curricula where knowledge and its application are integrated throughout the learning process there is still a real problem of transfer of medical problem-solving ability. The form in which students first encounter the medical problem and the way they go about tackling it has to closely resemble the form in which they will encounter and tackle the problem when they are practising physicians if there is to be a useful transfer of professional competence.

The practical implication of this transfer problem is that it is not sufficient to tack transferable skills on to conventional academic curricula – the skills simply won't transfer effectively to non-academic contexts. It is necessary to bring elements of the world of work into the classroom, to confront students with situations and problems which resemble those they will eventually have to tackle, and to allow them to learn the necessary skills in work-like contexts, tackling the problems in the way they will eventually have to tackle them outside academia. Learning to debate ideas in a seminar will not necessarily help a student to win an argument in a committee, to convince a client, to negotiate a contract or to represent a case in a court of enquiry. Learning to get good marks in an essay will not necessarily enable a graduate to write concise briefing notes for a boss, to write a tender for a contract or to get a magazine article published. Oral and written communication skills are not so general or generalisable. Academic skills needed for conventional undergraduate work may not even prepare students well for a subsequent life in academia, where the demands are quite unlike those faced in studying in the context of taught courses. The problem of transfer poses a much greater challenge to conventional

The extent to which skills transfer from one context to another depends on the similarity of the contexts.

It may be necessary to bring the world of work into the classroom if skills are to be learnt in an appropriate context.

4

curricula than simply having to drop a little from a lecture programme in order to fit in some time for skills. The curricula themselves have to be transformed if skills development is to be worthwhile. Examples of transformed curricula can be found in Section 6.

1.4 Are transferable skills discipline-specific?

Section 2 contains a general purpose list of transferable skills which is similar to that used in a number of Enterprise in Higher Education initiatives. Some of these skills take similar forms whatever the discipline, and similar levels of competence or sophistication are appropriate. For example teamwork skills are relevant in many contexts and in most of these contexts teamwork looks much the same and involves many of the same sub-skills.

Different disciplines are likely to value and embody some of the transferable skills to a different extent. Creative problem solving and interpersonal skills are commonly more highly valued in Business than in Science, for example. Also there are obviously wide differences of specialisation or sophistication in the nature and extent of use of skills between disciplines. What information technology skills mean to an engineer is likely to be rather more extensive than what it means to an art historian, but there will be a clear overlap in many areas such as word-processing and the use of remote databases. In languages the degree of skill may be far greater than in second language use for Business but the skills involved are still recognisably similar, though in a Modern Languages course the skills might be considered part of the discipline where in a Languages for Business course the same skills might be considered "transferable". In English there is a range of relatively specialist textual skills which would not normally be included in a written communication skills programme in Engineering, while in Civil Engineering the kinds of complex project management skills necessary to cope with major construction projects are beyond what is necessary to undertake research projects in English.

Specialisation may change the form skills take. In Cartography, Engineering Design, Publishing, Visual Media or Architecture the use of graphics software can be highly distinctive. The skills needed to use such software may have little in common with those needed to use the kinds of popular graphics software available for most microcomputers and used in introductory information technology courses.

In some subjects the form specific skills take may be rather distinctive and of limited relevance to other subjects. For example in Law written communication skills include drafting legal documents and oral communication skills include advocacy and negotiation. An adequate communications skills course appropriate for scientists would not equip lawyers with the skills they need at all well.

There seems to be a gradual shading from, at one extreme, transferable skills which are completely general and common to most endeavour, through specific forms of skills which are somewhat distinctive to the discipline, to the other extreme where the skills are almost entirely discipline-specific and may even be seen as part of the discipline rather than as transferable skills at all. How far a course chooses to move along this continuum from its traditional discipline-specific base is a matter of choice. It is not that some courses involve transferable skills while others do not, but that some have moved further along this continuum than others and transferable skills have a greater emphasis and a more central role.

What may seem an advanced or specialist skill in one discipline may be a basic skill in another.

But not in 'life skills'.

The form skills take may differ markedly from one discipline to another.

5

1.5 Institutional benefits and institutional policies

Paying serious attention to transferable skills is an expensive business. Does a concern for transferable skills carry costs without any benefits? It is clear that graduates value transferable skills and rate them as more useful than course content while they are in their first jobs. Prospective students are increasingly aware of the value of transferable skills and, through the style of teaching and learning at GCSE level, are increasingly experienced and sophisticated in transferable skills and expect learning processes to utilise them. Paying attention to these skills can have clear payoffs for institutions. Oxford Brookes University, for example, has the most employable graduates, with the lowest proportion of unemployed graduates, of 96 institutions (*Times Higher Education Supplement*, 14 May 1993). This reputation in turn attracts large numbers of good applicants. Such success does not come about purely through the idiosyncratic interest or application of individual lecturers, though initiatives may start there. What is required is a comprehensive range of institutional policies and support mechanisms.

Paying attention to students' transferable skills may improve employability.

Concern for skills development at Oxford Brookes University started with extensive study skills programmes in the late 70s. By the early 80s skills were being built into courses rather than taught separately and by the mid 80s some degree programmes had already adopted a comprehensive and integrated approach to the development of a range of transferable skills (see Jenkins and Pepper, 1988, for the approach taken in Geography). Concern for the development of transferable skills is now institutionalised in a variety of ways:

- New course proposals and periodic course reviews must include a review of the way the development of transferable skills is built into course design, delivery and assessment.

- Formal descriptions of modules, used for validation and course documentation, must contain an analysis of the transferable skills which are explicitly taught and assessed within each module (see Section 4.3).

- Degree programmes analyse where different skills are taught and assessed so as to produce a balanced and progressive approach across three years.

Clear institutional policies may be necessary if the development of transferable skills is to pervade students' experience.

- There is a formal policy that all students will leave the institution with a profile of their transferable skills, in addition to their transcript of modules taken and grades received. This has involved comprehensive changes in curricula, assessment methods and administrative record-keeping systems and the transformation of personal tutors into profiling tutors. Section 9 provides examples of profiling.

- Innovation is extensively funded, both through the Enterprise in Higher Education programme and through the existing Staff Release Scheme.

- Training in the development of transferable skills is provided for lecturers, both through a component of the Certificate in Teaching in Higher Education, which is compulsory for new lecturers, and through a variety of seminars, workshops, conferences, publications and other means for experienced lecturers.

6

1.6 Sampling

You may have on your shelves a 200-page manual concerning one specific skill for one specific audience: teamwork skills for managers, for example. But in this basic manual it is not possible to be comprehensive and deal with all skills or all possible contexts or types of course. Instead its purpose is to illustrate ways of going about the development of skills and to offer a variety of examples involving different skills in different contexts. It also attempts to highlight the crucial features of skills development: the structures of exercises, the principles of training, the ground rules for providing feedback, which can be applied to most situations whatever the skill or context involved.

1.7 The structure and contents of the manual

Section 2 concerns the identification of the transferable skills relevant to you and your students, and which of these skills it is most important to concentrate on.

Section 3 is about general principles of skills development, especially how skills are learnt through experience. It provides a checklist for reviewing skills training provision.

Section 4 builds on these general principles by identifying four key elements of skills development in the context of academic courses, the absence of any of which will weaken the effectiveness of efforts to develop skills: training, demand, monitoring and assessment. Each of the following four sections focuses on one of these four elements.

Section 5 provides examples of training exercises and materials, and highlights their important features.

Section 6 provides examples of the way Geography, Engineering and Hotel and Catering Management courses operate so as to demand the use of transferable skills.

Section 7 illustrates ways to monitor skill development and provide feedback to students on their skills.

Section 8 illustrates ways to assess skills, concentrating on teamwork and written communication skills.

Section 9 provides a brief introduction to the use of profiling as a way of structuring, recording and assessing skills development.

While this booklet cannot cover all skills in depth, it addresses issues which apply to the development of all skills.

LIVERPOOL JOHN MOORES UNIVERSITY
LEARNING SERVICES

Developing Students' Transferable Skills

1.7 The structure and contents of the manual

Skills review

2.1 Self-review

It may be difficult to develop skills in others which we lack ourselves, and many transferable skills may be outside the areas where we feel competent or confident. We may need to develop some of our own skills as part of the process of helping students to develop their skills. Use the checklist below to identify those skills you feel confident in, those you feel you lack, and those you would be interested in developing further.

Transferable skills	Examples
Communication	writing reports, giving presentations, using media (e.g. video, posters)
Group work	leadership, chairing, co-operation, teamwork
Personal	independence, autonomy, self-assessment, self-confidence
Interpersonal	influencing, counselling, listening, interviewing, assertiveness, negotiation
Organisational	time management, project management, objective-setting, project evaluation
Teaching and training	identifying learning needs, designing and running workshops, coaching, peer tutoring
Learning	reading flexibly and with purpose, note-taking flexibly and with purpose, literature search and review
Information gathering	locating information sources, evaluating sources and data, extracting relevant information, interpretation of data, presentation of data
Problem solving	problem analysis, creative problem solving, decision making
Language	oral skills, use of a foreign language
Information technology	using word-processing, databases, spread sheets, graphics, DTP.
Entrepreneurship	taking initiatives, seizing opportunities, creativity

We may lack the skills which we wish to develop in others.

9

Skills	Comments What are you good at? What do you feel less confident about? What specific skills would you like to develop for yourself?
Conclusions about your own transferable skills	

2.2 Student skills review

In order to identify which areas of skill to concentrate on it is useful to make three judgements about each skill area:

1   To what extent is this skill valuable to the learning of your subject?

2   To what extent is this skill valuable to students in the kinds of jobs they will go on to after they have studied your subject?

3   To what extent and to what level do your students already possess these skills?

Using the same list of skills, rate each in turn in relation to each of these questions, using the following rating scales. The higher the total score, the more attention you should be paying to the skills involved.

	Questions 1 and 2 1 = irrelevant 2 = not very valuable 3 = somewhat valuable 4 = valuable 5 = essential	**Question 3** 1 = all possess wide range of outstanding skills 2 = most possess range of good skills 3 = some possess some skills 4 = a few possess a few skills 5 = hardly any possess any skills	
Skills	**1: Value to students' study**	**2: Value to students' future work**	**3: Students' current skill level**	**Total**
Communication		5		
Group work		5		
Personal		5		
Interpersonal		5		
Organisational				
Teaching and training				
Learning				
Information gathering				
Numeracy				
Problem solving				
Language				
Information technology				
Entrepreneurship				

If it is not possible to develop all skills, which should be a high priority?

How are skills learnt?

3.1 The experiential learning cycle

Students do not become proficient in the use of a skill simply by being told about it, discussing it or thinking about it – they have to practise the skill. But practise, on its own, is also ineffective. It is necessary to notice what went well and not so well and to reflect on this and why it happened. It is necessary to develop an "informal theory" or personal explanation of what is going on and what being skillful consists of. And this informal theory needs to be used to help to make decisions next time about what to do differently. The learning of skills involves a four-stage cycle.

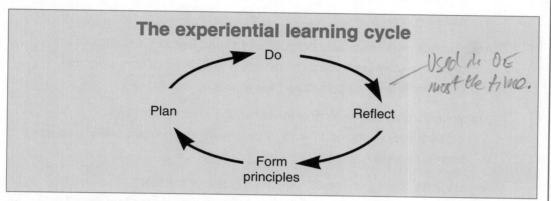

The experiential learning cycle

Do → Reflect → Form principles → Plan → Do

Used in OE most the time.

Skill learning involves a cyclical process which may need to be repeated many times.

This is the "experiential learning cycle", a model of how theory is related to practice in learning by doing. You can start anywhere you like on the cycle – with a new experience, with reflections on past experiences, with theory, or with planning to tackle a new situation – as long as you progress round the cycle in the right direction. Teaching and learning processes associated with each stage of the cycle are illustrated in the table below.

Stage	Illustrative learning activity
Do	Experiential exercises, actually using the skills, work placements
Reflect	Watching a video of yourself, discussing what happened, using a checklist to assess the use of a skill, keeping a reflective log or diary, profiling skills
Form	Listening to a lecture about a skill, reading, summarising general principles from a discussion.
Plan	Preparing for a presentation or for teamwork, setting action plans, identifying priorities for skills development using a profile

Ineffective skill development processes often emphasise one aspect of the learning cycle at the expense of the others.

In the light of this model of how skills are learnt, identify which aspects of the process are emphasised or under-emphasised in your courses? It is common, for example, for there to be opportunities to use skills (Do), but less common for there to be much reflection on how effectively these skills were used (Reflect), and even less common for general principles to be presented or derived from experience (Form principles). If you were to emphasise one aspect of this cycle to a greater extent in order to improve the learning of skills, which aspect would it be?

13

3.2 Skills development checklist

You may feel that you already put effort into developing a range of skills but that your efforts are not as effective or as comprehensive as you would like. The following checklist may help to diagnose where you might enhance your efforts, and can be used to review any skills development process.

- ☐ Do students feel the need to develop the skill?
  e.g. Do they care whether they have the skill? Do they realise the way professionals work?

- ☐ Are students given advice about using the skill?
  e.g. Are they briefed before the first time they use posters about what makes a clear poster?

- ☐ Are students given examples or models of expert use of the skill?
  e.g. Have they seen you demonstrate a skills? Have they seen an excellent project report before they write their own?

- ☐ Are students given some form of initial training in using the skill?
  e.g. Are they expected to work in groups without any prior exercises about teamwork skills?

- ☐ Are students given a chance to practise the use of the skill?
  e.g. Do they have several "trial runs" before they do the real thing?

- ☐ Is the practice 'safe' for students so that they can experiment?
  e.g. Are they assessed the very first time they use a skill? Can they get feedback in private rather than in front of the class?

- ☐ Are students encouraged to experiment and to take risks?
  e.g. Do assessment criteria include and value creativity and innovation?

- ☐ Is attention paid to the emotional climate in which skills are developed?
  e.g. Do students feel relaxed and safe about using and demonstrating the skill or anxious and exposed?

- ☐ Do students get feedback on the use of the skill?

- ☐ Do students get the chance to use the skill in different contexts?
  e.g. Do students write a variety of different types of report on work in teams of different size or on different types of task?

- ☐ Are students encouraged to follow a "recipe" in using a skill, or to become flexible?
  e.g. Do your students write all reports in the same way or do you see attempts at variety?

Other important questions you would want to add . . .

In the light of the above, what aspects of your teaching already fosters rapid skills development and what might you pay more attention to or do differently?

14

How can skills be developed in the context of academic courses?

4.1 Training, Demand, Monitoring, Assessment

Implementing effective skills development programmes involves four elements:

Training

If students lack a skill then they cannot suddenly use it, and students often start from such a low base-line that they need help before they can even start. If you are asking students to use a new skill, such as using posters to communicate, for the first time, it makes sense to start with some training. As training processes involve experience, it can sometimes be interesting to start with an experience "from cold": for example, trying to produce an effective poster without help. This will highlight the extent of students' learning needs and may reveal some skills transferred from other situations and knowledge of posters from having seen plenty of examples. However, it can also be very discouraging. Students' first posters, just like their first attempts at teamwork or their first oral presentations, can be depressingly bad. Students should not be left to struggle for long before being trained.

> It can discourage students to expect them to use and exhibit skills they don't have.

Demand

Students need to practise skills. Courses need to make demands on students that give them that practice. Following a training session on communicating with posters, Psychology students could be required to present their next experimental work on a poster and present the poster at the next lab session. Such poster sessions could become regular, even weekly, events. The issue of demand is related to the issue of "time on task". Students need to have learning time allocated to the development of the skill. If you simply tell students that they should spend time on developing their skills it probably will not happen. The easiest way to get students to spend time on their skills is to allocate class time, to set assignments and to devise learning activities which involve the use of the skills.

> Course demands may need to be changed so as to require the use of skills.

Monitoring

Skills seldom develop suddenly or in one go. Most skills development does not take place in training exercises but afterwards: skills continue to develop gradually over a long period. Students progressively "tune up" their skills. They do this primarily through noticing what works and what doesn't, experimenting and getting feedback on the consequences. Students who lack skill also lack any way of noticing what works or judging effectiveness. Students need ways of monitoring their effectiveness and they need to get into the habit of reviewing their effectiveness. Among the most useful materials in this manual are the checklists which students can use to monitor and self-assess their own performance. In areas such as teamwork, where social conventions tend to obstruct open review of performance, such checklists can be particularly helpful.

> Improvement requires feedback; if you do not have the time to give students feedback, then they need to learn to give it to themselves.

Assessment

Assessment is the most powerful lever you have to influence what students pay attention to.

Students can be very strategic, noticing what counts and what is rewarded. Given the excessive size of most curricula, reading lists and so on they need to be "selectively negligent", choosing what to leave out. This is in itself a valuable transferable skill and students who lack this awareness of cues as to what counts in courses are likely to fare badly. Most conventional assessment processes do not indicate to students that skills matter. If you want students to take skills seriously then you need to assess them.

Also, if we are serious about the role of skills in our curricula, then students' grades and degree classifications should indicate something about how skilful they are, and not just something about what they know.

If any one of the elements is missing then there can be severe consequences. We have seen a course in which the demands on students to use skills were considerable: in their first term students had to work in teams of eight to study a small business. Through this they were supposed to develop teamwork skills. All that they discovered was that teams can be hell. Without any initial training in teamwork the students lacked a way of making progress.

We have seen communication skills courses which contained excellent training exercises but which were followed by content-oriented courses which made almost no demand on students to display their skills, which then fell into disuse.

Courses sometimes go to the trouble of some initial skills training and then make demands on students to use these skills, but provide no follow-up support. Although the demand is there, students are not encouraged to pay attention to developing the application of the skill. An obvious example might be essay writing or lab report writing, where students can continue making the same kinds of errors and using the same ineffective approaches to writing despite lots of practice, simply because they are never encouraged to stop and reflect on their writing and to experiment with alternative approaches. Practice alone does not make perfect.

A lack of assessment can undermine otherwise well thought out skills development initiatives. For example, students can be trained in teamwork skills, can be required to work in teams, and can take part in regular workshops designed to help them to improve the effective operation of their teams. However, if the assessment consists of an individual report or a conventional exam, then students have no incentive to take teamwork seriously and are likely to concentrate on private, competitive study. If skills are not assessed then students soon stop taking the skill, and skills development exercises and courses, seriously.

Assessment on its own will achieve little without training, demand and monitoring.

Assessment is probably the single most powerful tool you have to orient students' time and effort towards the skills which matter, but it is still insufficient on its own. For example, we know of a course which assessed students' project work using a videotape report. Students were required to present to a static camera and all the tutor saw of their project work was the ten-minute video. This was intended to develop students' skills in handling the medium: a good idea in principle. However, the students had not been trained in video presentation techniques, did not practise them during the project and did not monitor their own skill. In fact the assessment was the first time the students had ever presented to camera! Their videos did not demonstrate much skill and all students learnt was that presenting to camera is intimidating and jolly difficult.

Sometimes students' skills are repeatedly assessed without there being any

16

noticeable improvement. This is common where tutorial comments are either very limited, or are solely concerned with content. Ideally assessment should provide students with feedback and there should be mechanisms which encourage students to reflect on this feedback and modify their practices. This might involve students' marking exercises and self-assessment.

4.2 TDMA course review checklist

Use this checklist to identify which aspects of skill development are built into the way the degree programme or course you teach on develops enterprise skills. You are likely to have to look at course review documents and to ask around, as there may be no coherent approach to skill development and much skill development work may be implicit and informal. You should be able to identify which of the four aspects of skill development needs most attention. It may well be in the area of training and assessment rather than in the area of demand.

Skills	Training	Demand	Monitoring	Assessment
Communication				
Group work				
Personal				
Interpersonal				
Organisational				
Teaching and training				
Learning				
Information gathering				
Numeracy				
Problem solving				
Language				
Information technology				
Entrepreneurship				
Conclusions:				

Do your courses make demands where there has been no training?

Do you pay the same kind of attention to each skill?

17

4.3 Describing the skills content of curricula

A concern for both the teaching and assessment of skills may be built into course documentation. At Oxford Brookes University module descriptions include a grid that identifies which of a basic list of skills are explicitly taught and assessed (as opposed to simply being used), as in the example below.

How do students on your courses know which skills are involved?

Module 5272   The Culture of Publishing

General skills

At the end of the module the student will have practised the following skills:

Skill	Taught	Assessed
Communication skills		
- report writing		
- verbal communication		
- presentation		•
Learning skills		
- information gathering		•
- independent work		•
Problem-solving skills	•	
New technology skills		•
Number skills		
Group work skills		•
Organisational skills	•	•
Personal skills		

Learning experiences

The module will engage the student in the following types of learning experience:

Group project work

Group presentation

Independent learning

Use of new technology

Case studies

Peer-assessment

Teaching and learning time

Student/teacher contact time 27 hours:

9 hours   lectures

18 hours   seminars/workshops

Additionally students should be expected to spend 93 hours studying:

10 hours   group work

25 hours   seminar reading and preparation

20 hours   assignment preparation

20 hours   background reading

18 hours   diary

Is there time for students to develop and use these skills?

18

Examples of transferable skills training exercises

5.1 Introduction

In a short general guide to developing transferable skills it is not possible to be comprehensive but only to illustrate types of exercises that have certain key features. These key features are:

Economy

All these exercises are designed to be economical of the lecturer's time. They are either capable of being run with quite large classes (for example, 5.2.2 was run with an entire first-year intake of 80) or are designed for autonomous student use in the context of large workshop-type sessions or outside class. Even detailed experiential exercises involving the practice of specific small-scale skills may need no supervision (as with 5.4). Students are perfectly capable of running through these exercises independently.

Developing skills need not be expensive.

Low demand on expertise

None of these exercises require much in the way of expertise from the lecturer – either expertise in the skill concerned or expertise in running skills sessions. Instead they rely on students' experience, checklists and clear instructions.

Use of students' experience

Most of the exercises generate experiences which students can then reflect on: they try creating a team (5.2.1), practising group seminar presentations (5.3.1) or influencing others (5.4). These experiences are reflected upon and learning points are extracted. Some of the exercises also draw on students' past experiences, as in the early stages of the exercise in 5.3.1.

Clear criteria

In order to analyse the experiences or to judge performances it is useful to have clear criteria (as in 5.3.3) or explicit checklists (as in 5.2.1). It is possible to get students to generate their own criteria (as in 5.3.1), though this may take more time and be much messier to handle in large groups. It may be neater to start with your criteria and move on to student criteria once they have more experience.

Clear advice

Students sometimes, and with some justification, claim that learning transferable skills is like the blind leading the blind. If the lecturer has little expertise in the skill and the students have little experience then advice and criteria generated purely through an experiential exercise can appear flimsy and unconvincing. The exercise in 5.2.1, for example, can operate without the lists of advice, but tends to produce rather few insights unless a good deal of time is set aside for debriefing. And without the advice most groups have only learnt how not to become an effective team when the time runs out. If you have limited time, limited expertise and

Students need clear guidelines or advice.

students with limited experience, then give clear advice. The advice in 5.3.2 may lead to less profound learning than the exercise in 5.3.1, but it may nevertheless improve presentations faster and it uses no classroom time. It is possible, of course, to use experiential exercises and clear written advice together.

Experimentation

Many transferable skills involve behaving differently from the habitual patterns we have established. In order to change and improve it is necessary to go beyond fine tuning or trying out minor techniques and to experiment with completely new ways of behaving. In 5.4, for example, students are invited to identify patterns of behaviour they do not normally use and to experiment with these patterns through a series of short exercises. In many of the exercises in this section of the manual there is an element of simply trying things out to see what it feels like and to see what happens. To encourage this kind of open experimentation it is important to preserve privacy (as in small groups, with no reporting back) and reduce risk (by, for example, allowing plenty of opportunity for experimentation before anything is assessed or contributes to assessment marks).

Practice

Students don't learn skills by listening or reading about them and they don't learn them in one go. It takes practice. I once encountered a Chemistry degree course which claimed that it attended to presentation skills because it provided one opportunity in the second year. The reality is that most of us are still working on our lecturing skills after twenty years, and which of us ever really gets on top of time management? Learning most transferable skills is a life-long process and it takes a great deal of practice to improve. A single opportunity doesn't help much. If you only have the opportunity for one exercise on a particular skill, try and build in the opportunity for two attempts – perhaps a quick trial run and then a serious attempt – in order to go round the experiential learning cycle (see 3.1) more than once. Some of the exercises here look complex (as with 5.3.1.) but this is partly to give students a variety of opportunities.

Feedback

It is a fundamental principle of skill learning that you need feedback to improve. Practice without feedback can be almost totally ineffective. Most of these exercises involve students in giving each other feedback on a brief opportunity to demonstrate a skill (as in 5.4). Section 8.2 includes a form used during assessment of essays which structures the way feedback is provided. Section 7.1 provides guidelines for giving and receiving open-ended oral feedback, and Section 7.3 offers a form for giving feedback on seminar presentations.

5.2 Teamwork skills

Y ou cannot expect students to start work immediately in teams and to operate effectively from the start. They need time allocated to form and establish their team. They need to pay attention to:

- getting to know each other, including individual strengths and weaknesses and preferences for working in a team;

- identifying the roles and responsibilities of individuals within the team;

- establishing ground rules for behaviour within the team;

- clarifying the team's goals and tasks;

- scheduling tasks, meetings and deadlines;

- learning to use different group methods for meetings.

Three manuals are available from the Oxford Centre for Staff Development on teamwork: a brief guide for students, a substantial manual for student teams, and a tutor guide. The brief guide elaborates on ten pieces of advice:

1	Be clear what the project is all about
2	Be selective about who you work with
3	Take the trouble to build a real team
4	Decide how you'd like it to be
5	Make sure someone is doing it
6	Divide the project up and share it out
7	Have proper meetings, not disorganised chats
8	Discuss how it is going
9	Give each other feedback – gently
10	Plan your team presentation carefully

5.2.1 Becoming a team

The checklists below can be used in fast and fun exercises to establish teams and working relationships within them. A very simple 60-minute exercise involves the following steps and can be run with up to 100 students.

Asking students to become a team can highlight what is special about teams and what steps they need to take.

- Quickly cluster into teams of [whatever size team you want to use].

- You have 30 minutes to form your cluster into a functioning team. You can do anything you like which you think will make you a team. (Display or hand out the two checklists either at the start or after ten minutes.)

What you can do to avoid becoming a team

don't join in

have an aimless chat

allow an individual to dominate

allow members not to join in

keep it formal, neutral and abstract

avoid any expression of feelings

refuse to set yourself any task or goal

don't find out about each other

don't disclose anything about yourself

express criticism and hostility towards others

don't listen to each other

What you can do to form a team

get to know each other

do something social together

do something risky together

carry out a task together

do something physical together

disclose personal information about yourself

express feelings about being in the team

identify your strengths and potential shortcomings as a team

identify your skills which may be useful to the team

identify your preferences about how you like to work with others

build, make, construct, draw something together

do something creative (write a two-minute play?) together

sing a song together

play a game (consequences) together

be private (even secretive) together

be 'better' than the other team

- Ask teams to discuss "In what way are you a team now which you were not before? How did you achieve this? In what sense are you not yet a team? What could you do next to become a fully effective team?" Ask several of the teams to report in public on their discussions.

The following exercise was run to develop seminar groups as teams at the start of their first year on an Italian course.

5.2.2 Seminar group training session

Aims
To introduce students to each other

To establish effective seminar groups

To develop effective working practice

To develop seminar presentation skills

To establish methods of giving feedback to seminar presenters to improve their presentations

Programme

10.00 Introduction

10.10 Team formation
Establishment of tutorial groups of eight and a team-building exercise in which students had 30 minutes in which to turn themselves from an anonymous cluster into a functioning team.

10.40 Doing it wrong . . .
A negative brainstorm and discussion of how to make seminars dreadful, helped by second- and third-year students, followed by a display of posters.

11.00 Coffee

11.20 Doing it right . . . Ground rules
Groups discuss the opposite of how to make seminars dreadful in order to establish the ground rules they wish to work to. Each group displays and signs their own set of ground rules on a poster.

12.00 Effective presentations and discussions
A very brief presentation based on a handout

12.20 Preparation for seminars in the afternoon
Each pair in the tutorial groups of eight will have the chance to give a 20-minute seminar: ten minutes presentation and ten minutes discussion, followed by five minutes feedback. The pairs have until 2.20 to prepare.

2.20 Practice seminar

2.20	first seminar pair
2.45	second seminar pair
3.10	third seminar pair
3.35	fourth seminar pair

4.00   Tea

4.20   Closing exercise

Each person in turn completes one of the following the sentences:
"Something I'm going to do to make my tutorial group work well is . . ."
"How I feel about being in my tutorial group is . . ."
"Something we have learnt as a group is . . ."

4.30   Close

Students often find it easier to describe how to fail and go wrong than how to succeed!

23

5.3   Presentation skills

5.3.1 Presentation skills training exercise

This is a training exercise designed to highlight and demonstrate the skills of effective group presentation. It requires student groups to make brief presentations on effective and ineffective group presentations. It assumes that most students make a group presentation as a formal course requirement. Originally developed for trainee district nurses and access students in Physics, this exercise can be adapted to very different courses or used as a model to develop an exercise that better suits your students' needs. It requires about an hour and a half.

Students know from experience, largely through what they have seen teachers do, what makes for an effective or ineffective presentation. However, they may well not have reviewed that experience systematically and applied it to making their own presentations effective. Nor are they likely to have practised and internalised the necessary skills. After they have done an exercise such as the one described here it may be useful to refer them to written guides on effective presentations, to show them training videos and to develop exercises on particular aspects of giving a presentation, such as using the overhead projector.

Even if students have never given a presentation they have listened to hundreds and can tell the difference between a good one and a bad one.

How to give an effective group presentation

(The key instructions given to students orally or on the overhead projector are in italics.)

1   Divide the class into groups – it may well be appropriate for these to be the same groups that are to give a formal presentation later in the course. (The description that follows assumes groups of four students, with about 30 in the class.) Ensure they are sitting where they can readily talk to each other and are away from other groups.

2   Remind them that the course requires them to make an effective group presentation.

     The aims of this exercise are to:

     • *clarify why this course uses group presentations;*

     • *review your experience of what makes for an effective group presentation;*

     • *give you experience of making a group presentation;*

     • *develop guidelines for giving effective presentations in this course.*

3   *In your groups decide which of you is an A, B, C, and a D.*

4   Remind them, or if necessary tell them how to brainstorm.

     For this section of the exercise I want A to chair, B to be scribe . Brainstorm why you think group presentations are an important part of this course . Then agree on three principal reasons. You have till . . .

5   Get three or four groups to give one principal reason. Get one of the students to write them on a flip-chart. Then you state your three principal reasons for making group presentations a course requirement. It is better

24

at this stage not to get into questions and explanations on the details of the course requirements, but if necessary reassure the students that you will deal with this later .

6   *For this section of the exercise B is to chair, C is scribe. Think back over the group presentations you have seen or done yourself. Brainstorm as many ways as possible to make them totally ineffective. Then agree on five principal ways to make a group presentation ineffective. You have till . . .*

7   *C is now chair, D is scribe. Now brainstorm ways to make group presentations effective. Then agree on five principal ways to make a group presentation effective. You have till . . .*

8   Divide the groups into two sets; one you designate as being responsible for effective group presentations, the other for ineffective presentations.

9   *D is responsible for chairing this stage. I suggest you also appoint a scribe and a time-keeper. As a group you should:*

     • *go back to your five basic rules (for either effective or ineffective presentations); do you now want to amend them?*

     • *at [state a time] you should be ready to come to the front and make a group presentation:*

          - one of you will state the rule;

          - another person or persons will act out the rule;

          - after this those who have not spoken so far will answer questions from the audience on the value of the rule or how to ensure that it is carried out;

          - as a group, you are responsible for different people taking on different roles for each rule.

10   Depending on the numbers of groups and the time available you will have to adjust how you proceed. First call on the groups responsible for ineffective presentations. In turn each gives a presentation on one rule. Those who come later are told that they should choose a rule they have developed but which is different from those that have preceded them. You then call on the groups responsible for effective presentations to go through the same procedure.

11   Your role is to set things up clearly, to act as chair (or designate someone else to do that) and to be as unobtrusive as possible. Students have to feel they are centre stage.

12   After all groups have performed you could clarify any student uncertainties about course requirements. After an exercise such as this students will ask much more penetrating questions. Again it can be valuable to require groups to specify the three (or four!) questions they want you to answer.

13   When you have answered these questions, ensure you give the groups time in this class period to reflect on their experience and plan for when they will give a formal presentation in the course.

Variations include (i) reminding students at the beginning of the exercise how presentations are to be assessed and your criteria for assessment; (ii) negotiating the criteria they think appropriate; (iii) asking students to specify the aspects of presentation skills they need to work on and perhaps where they want further training.

5.3.2 Advice to students on seminar presentations

The following extract from a handout to students illustrates the kinds of realistic practical advice it is possible to give with the intention of improving the quality of seminar presentations.

Advice should be direct, specific and realistic.

Seminar Presentation Mistakes

These guidelines identify the common mistakes students make in seminar presentations and suggests how to avoid them.

1 Forgetting there is an audience

A presentation does not only involve your speaking, it also involves your audience's listening. Why should your audience bother to listen to what you have to say? You have to interest them at the start and find ways of making them listen. Think about what might intrigue them, puzzle them, contradict their expectations, be controversial or entertaining. Think about what they already know and how they could relate that to what you have to offer. Think about your audience, not just about your material.

2 Including too much content

Inexperienced presenters almost always have too much material to present, and rush through it, overburdening their audience and still taking too long. 20 minutes is the limit on most people's concentration, even when the presentation is riveting. Cut down your content and slow down on your rate of presentation. If you are worried about running out of material either time yourself (presenting at an even pace into a mirror), or give yourself time-fillers such as extra examples, something for the audience to read, or questions for the audience to answer and discuss part-way through your presentation.

3 Lack of direction

It is difficult for an audience to listen to a presenter for long if they don't know where you are going with your talk, or why. You need to explain, at the start, what they are in for and where you will take them. It isn't much help just saying: "Today is about X". You need to explain how you will tackle X and what you will spend time on. For example, "My presentation today is about X. What interests me about this is the question of Y. I'd like to look at this question in three ways, A, B and C, and illustrate these with examples drawn from Z. The second of these is the most interesting and I'll be spending longest on this."

4   Lack of structure

Your audience will get lost if you don't give them a map of where you are going. For example, "I've chosen three texts to analyse to illustrates my points, X, Y and Z. I'll use the first two to show how . . . and the third to contrast that with . . . After each text I'll summarise my points." It can be helpful to give some signposts along the way to show them where you have got to and where you will be going next. For example, "So I've looked at this first text and shown how . . . by giving examples of . . . and now I'm going to . . . before going on to . . ."

5   Nothing to look at

It is hard just to listen to someone. People find it easier when they have something to look at too. Provide your audience with handouts (containing a summary of your seminar, extracts from texts or crucial passages from your central sources). Use a whiteboard or blackboard to summarise your points or illustrate what you are talking about. Show flip-chart sheets prepared beforehand, which provide an overview, a map, a diagram. Use an overhead projector and prepare transparencies on each of your main points. Give your audience something to look at while you are talking.

6   Nothing to do

Just listening is dull. It is more interesting if the audience have something more active to do. This might involve reading a passage, analysing a text, solving a problem, suggesting alternative ways to interpret or analyse a passage or historical event, suggesting examples of a phenomenon or illustrations of a literary device or genre and so on. From time to time, give your audience some work to do.

7   Only note-taking

People won't join in, or even think very much, if they are furiously taking notes. Provide a handout so that your audience can concentrate on what you have to say.

8   No questions

If you talk non-stop, especially if you avoid eye contact with your audience, they are unlikely to ask you questions, even if they have questions in their mind. You need to invite questions. You can do this by saying at the start: "Please stop me to ask questions or seek clarification." You can stop and invite questions: "Before I go on, is there anything you'd like to ask or for me to clarify?" You can stop and look round, inviting interruptions with your body language. Leave plenty of time even though the silence may feel threatening – it takes time to formulate questions. If none of these work, stop and ask people to write down two questions they would really like answered, give them a minute, and then take each person in turn and get them to read out one of their questions.

27

9 No questioning

Involve and challenge your audience by asking them questions. Prepare questions in advance. Don't ask "closed" questions, to which there is a right and wrong answer ("Who wrote . . . ?" "Did . . . write this before or after . . . ?") but open questions which can start a discussion ("What might be the problems of this way of looking at things?" "Is this the only way of seeing this?" "What is your opinion on this?").

10 No summary

When you have finished, don't just suddenly stop and say: "Well . . . that's it really." Summarise what you have said and make it clear what the key points were. Make sure your audience leave with a clear overview.

11 No discussion

Don't expect a discussion to happen all on its own. Make it clear that you want some discussion: "Let's stop for a few minutes to discuss this before I go on." Use body language to indicate that you are not about to start presenting again: sit down, relax, sit back, put your notes down. Think about what people might be interested in talking about and make suggestions: "I thought it might be interesting to explore . . . Do you think . . . or . . . ?" You can raise these issues at the start so that people are thinking about them while you are talking, and ready to join in when it is time to discuss.

12 Not drawing on what your audience know

People think more if they can relate what you are saying to what they know. Find out at the start what people have read and what they are familiar with and adjust your presentation accordingly. There is nothing more boring than going over ground everyone is already familiar with or dealing with something so outside everyone's experience that they can't relate to it. Half-way through ask: "What else have people read which addresses these issues?"

13 Reading out notes in full

Inexperienced presenters write out their presentation in full and read it out word for word. This is very dull for the audience and it isn't much fun for the presenter either. Experienced presenters rely on much briefer notes which give them an overview and a way of seeing very quickly what they are supposed to be talking about and what is coming next. Methods include:

• index cards which each contain one key idea or subsection of the presentation;

• a handout for the audience which the presenter uses as a framework for the talk;

• transparencies which summarise the key points and which the presenter uses to remind herself;

• very brief skeleton notes containing only single words or phrases which provide clues about the content.

You should aim to be able to look up at your audience most of the time, and to give the impression of thinking while you are talking.

14 No follow-up

If the seminar is the last time anyone thinks about your topic, then no-one will learn much. Make suggestions about where your audience might read about your topic. Give references and suggest which ones are worth looking at and which parts are most interesting. Tell them where not to bother and what to avoid. Suggest what you'd have been interested to look at next, if you'd had time.

15 No fun

Seminars don't have to be straight-faced and deadly serious. There will be more energy and involvement if people are enjoying themselves. Give yourself permission, and your audience permission, to relax and have a laugh.

16 No responsiveness or flexibility

Things don't always work out the way you thought. If you are way over people's heads or boring them to tears by going too fast, don't just plod on regardless. Stop and make sensible decisions about how to continue ("What should I explain first if the rest of this is going to make sense to you?" "Would it be helpful if I stopped for a minute and let you catch up and ask some questions?").

17 No improvement

It is not possible to be brilliant at giving presentations the first time. But you can learn and improve if you find out what went well and what could be changed. Ask your audience, or ask your tutor: "What do you think I did well in my presentation and what would you suggest I improved for next time?" Use the short questionnaire on page 30 to get your audience to give you feedback.

LIVERPOOL JOHN MOORES UNIVERSITY
LEARNING SERVICES

Developing Students' Transferable Skills

5.3.3 Assessing presentations

It is vital that the skills you care about and are trying to develop are also valued explicitly in your assessment scheme. The specific features of presentations you want students to display should be brought to students' attention through the use of criteria and rating scales. The presentation feedback form illustrated in Section 7.3 labels three points on each scale. The seminar assessment form below is used to allocate marks under four headings – two concerned with the subject matter and two concerned with process and skills. Students will need to discuss what a "2" or a "4" mean and practise using these scales if they are to be meaningful or reliable.

You may have different criteria for your students' presentations but you might still be able to use this format for assessment forms.

Seminar Assessment Criteria

20% of the marks for the course are awarded for each of two seminar presentations, which you share with your seminar partner. These marks are awarded by the audience at each seminar. Please assess your colleagues' seminar presentations using this form. Think about each criterion separately and thoughtfully rather than giving one global snap judgement. Add comments explaining your marks under each criterion and some helpful comments at the end. Complete the form immediately at the end of the seminar and hand it in to your tutor.

Seminar presenters: 1 .... 2 ....

Criterion	Mark					
Content: clarity of argument, understanding, explanation, overview, conclusions. Comments:	0	1	2	3	4	5
Sources: breadth and relevance, acknowledgement of sources, references, reading list. Comments:	0	1	2	3	4	5
Presentation: voice, use of a.v. aids, pace, variety, liveliness, handouts. Comments:	0	1	2	3	4	5
Discussion: involvement of group, questioning, answering, use of discussion methods. Comments:	0	1	2	3	4	5

Best things about the seminar.

What you should pay attention to next time.   Total Mark

30

5.4 Influencing skills

The ability to persuade someone else to listen, to agree, or to change a habit or course of action is one which often eludes us when we most need it. Sometimes this is because we have a limited repertoire and assume that our customary technique, be it bullying, reasoning or beguiling, is the only way simply because other ways do not form part of our repertoire. Also most of us know what other people do that causes us to resist their entreaties.

This training exercise offers a chance for students to check their repertoire of influencing skills and to extend it through practical exercises in a group. Simply hand them this and the following five pages and all you have to do is to keep them within reason to the time schedule.

Developing skills may involve widening our repertoire rather than tuning up an existing skill.

Student groups can often work completely independently if they have clear instructions like these.

Procedure

1 Individually, complete the influencing styles questionnaire as honestly as you can. This is for your own personal learning and does not have to be seen by anyone in authority! (5 minutes)

2 Now go through your responses and pick out which of the four styles you would like to do most work on or develop for yourself. You may like to choose a style which you don't use often, or feel uncomfortable about using. (2 minutes)

3 Pair up with another participant, find out which style they have chosen and ask them about how they see themselves in relation to it. (10 minutes)

4 Now form groups of four to six in such a way that there is a range of styles to be tried out in each group.

5 Take turns to select one of the 22 exercises on offer. This series of exercises provides a wide range of opportunities for students to try out behaviour which is not part of their normal repertoire. The exercises are designed to give you an opportunity to focus on one particular style. Each exercise will take between two and ten minutes. Allow at least ten minutes for feedback.*

6 The observers will note what you do and what impact you have on them and will give you feedback at the end of the exercise.

7 In addition to considering how you felt adopting a particular style, you can also review your reactions to the styles adopted by others.

*You may find it helpful to use the sheet "Giving and Receiving Feedback" in Section 7.1.

Which of the four influencing styles would you benefit most from working on?

Influencing styles: a Personal Questionnaire	Doing OK	Could do more	Could do less
Carrot and stick			
Evaluating; praising and criticising; giving the impression of sitting in judgment on others			
Communicating demands and requirements letting others know what you want; telling others what you will and will not go along with or accept			
Making position statements, using moral imperatives – should, ought, must			
Offering bargains, rewards, threats or punishments			
Using pressure tactics, status and authority			
Bridge-building			
Being open about your motives, intentions and reactions			
Admitting mistakes and errors without defensiveness			
Being prepared to show weakness, indecision, lack of strength			
Drawing out the intentions and goals of others			
Appreciating others' problems and difficulties			
Showing trust and confidence in others			
Testing and expressing your understanding of others' positions			
Visioning			
Showing your enthusiasm by tone of voice, gestures and use of words			
Using imagery to generate excitement in others			
Helping others to imagine a better future			
Appealing to common values, hopes and aspirations			
Building solidarity, generating a shared identity			
Reason and logic			
Putting forward opinions and ideas			
Taking the initiative to suggest solutions to problems			
Making proposals which are "open" and do not seek a prescribed response			
Giving reasons, arguments, facts to support your own position			
Expressing agreement or disagreement based on reason, logic or opinion			

32

5.4.1 Carrot and stick exercises

These exercises will provide experience in making others take account of a student's demands and wishes and in asserting their own needs. They also offer practice in using pressures and incentives and engaging in "tough bargaining".

Student's may learn most by selecting the exercise which looks hardest and most out of character.

Exercise 1

The other members of the group will engage in a conversation and will ignore you. Use assertive behaviour to make them include you. (Make sure you stick to "Carrot and stick" behaviours!)

Exercise 2

You have three minutes to persuade another group member to do something which would be good for them (e.g. skip a meal, give up smoking or drinking for a day, take some exercise, etc.). Use a high-pressure style. The other person may resist but if persuaded, must actually carry out the action to which they agreed.

Exercise 3

Identify a specific authority figure in your life (parent, teacher, boss) who has not treated you as you want or expect to be treated. Choose a group member to play the role of this authority figure and tell them how you are to be treated from now on. Demand specific changes in their behaviour. The "authority figure" may respond.

Exercise 4

Positively evaluate a member of your work group. Tell them what you expect from people and how they have met your standards.

Exercise 5

Find another group member who is willing to bargain with you. Each of you put £1 on the floor. You have four minutes to agree on an unequal division of the £2 based on which one of you has contributed or will contribute most to the group's learning today. If you have not reached agreement within four minutes, the observers will give feedback to both participants, after which they will award the whole £2 to the stronger bargainer.

Observer guide

Note such behaviours as:

1. Being in control of the situation, maintaining the initiative, not getting sidetracked.

2. Forcing own agenda and structure.

3. Stating goals, expectations and standards forcefully and succinctly.

4. Making strong, direct, evaluative statements, positive and /or negative, based on own standards.

5. Avoiding tentative words and phrases (e.g. "I hope . . .", "I wish . . .", "Maybe . . .") and qualifiers (e.g. "Sometimes . . .", "I think . . .", "From my perspective . . .").

5.4.2 Bridge-building exercises

These exercises will provide experience in generating trust, openness and involvement. "Active listening" is an important feature of this style, as it requires testing and expressing an understanding of others.

Exercise 1

Pick out a group member whom you particularly trust, even though you may not know the person well. Tell them why you trust them.

Exercise 2

Tell each group member something about them which you would like to get to know better.

Exercise 3

Tell the group something about yourself which would help them to understand you better but which is difficult for you to say. One group member should volunteer to respond to you by using "Effective Listening" skills.

Exercise 4

Take five minutes to find out from the group members their happiest experiences OR their greatest failures. Use "Effective Listening" skills.

Exercise 5

Express your views briefly (two minutes) on a controversial topic about which you feel strongly. Be prepared to disclose your deeper feelings on this issue. The other group members will then spend four minutes telling you how and why they disagree with you. You are allowed to respond only by clarifying, summarising, paraphrasing to indicate you have really heard and understood the others' criticisms. You are not allowed to respond by counter-argument.

Exercise 6

Identify a person in the group who makes you most uncomfortable and tell him or her why. Work with that person to reduce your own discomfort.

Observer guide

Note such behaviours as:

1   Sincerity, openness, non-defensiveness and spontaneity.

2   Intent listening, accurate reflection of others' problems and opinions.

3   Non-evaluative listening – absence of "oughts" or "shoulds".

4   Manner and tone implying acceptance of other person.

5.4.3 Visioning exercises

These exercises will provide experience in presenting ideas, proposals and capabilities in an exciting, convincing and positive way.

Exercise 1

Assume that the other group members are a silent committee which will make a decision whether or not to employ you. Decide what job you are seeking. Describe your potential, contributions and the exciting possibilities that can be realised if you are employed.

Exercise 2

Share with the group a hope or dream you have for the future. Try to fill them with excitement about your vision.

Exercise 3

Use "visioning" to persuade another member to do something which would be good for them (e.g. skip a meal, give up smoking or drinking for a day, take some exercise, etc.) The other person may resist. Do not meet this resistance with pressure but try to involve them with your enthusiasm and concern for their well-being.

Exercise 4

Share, with images and feelings, one of the most happy periods, events or experiences in your life.

Exercise 5

Tell the group how you feel your choice of course is significant and meaningful – how it reflects values which you believe are important.

Observer guide

Note such behaviours as:

1   Articulation of "exciting possibilities" with enthusiasm.

2   Use of imagery, "word pictures".

3   Involvement of others by identifying shared dreams and values, common interests.

4   Communication of enthusiasm, excitement, commitment by non-verbal means – gestures, body movement, facial expressions, tone of voice, etc.

When listening to feedback, use the guidelines on page 47.

Developing Students' Transferable Skills

5.4.4 Reason and logic exercises

These exercises will provide experience in presenting and defending ideas and proposals in a rational and logical way.

Exercise 1

Assume that the other group members are a silent committee which will make a decision whether or not to employ you. Decide what job you are seeking. State what you can do for them and back up your assertions with fact and logic.

Exercise 2

Get another group member to take the role of an actual person with whom you work (e.g. boss, subordinate, customer, client, colleague etc.). Identify one or more things that person is doing (or not doing) which is significantly reducing your productivity/effectiveness. Convince the person to change their behaviour.

Exercise 3

Ask another member to compete with you in convincing the group that you will get the most out of today. Each of you has two minutes for your persuasive presentation, followed by one minute to rebut the arguments of the other. The group will decide the winner.

Exercise 4

Using reason, facts and logic, persuade another member to do something which would be good for them (e.g. skip a meal, give up smoking or drinking for a day, take some exercise, etc.). The other person may resist. Deal with the resistance by using reason and logic and by bringing as much evidence to bear as you can.

Exercise 5

Pick an object on your person or in the room which might have value to another member. Choose somebody and try to sell them the object, stressing its qualities, utility or advantages to the buyer. You may ask questions of the prospective buyer to determine their needs.

Exercise 6

Express your views on a topic where you have considerable knowledge. Explain to the group what reasons you have for your point of view. Others may question you.

Observer guide

Note such behaviours as:

1   Using well-structured and ordered argument.

2   Logical linking of points and examples.

3   Use of examples and illustrations, contrasting advantages and
           disadvantages.

4   Avoidance of emotive phrases, personal attacks, etc.

Observers should use the feedback guidelines on page 47.

36

Examples of courses demanding the use of transferable skills

6.1 Teamwork and communication skills in Geography

Brief description

The Geography field at Oxford Brookes University have developed courses in which students learn and develop skills as an integral part of learning Geography. With time, these skills have been integrated into a student programme so that skills introduced into the year one course are progressively developed to a higher level in courses in years two and three. Group work and spoken communication skills are two of the key skills developed.

Examples of courses incorporating skills

Below are brief snapshot descriptions of three courses that incorporate group work and spoken presentations.

In a course on political geography, groups of students tell their fellow students about the impact of present government policy on the geography of Britain. Their presentation may take the form of a speech, a simulated television programme or a playlet. A few days afterwards, each group meets with its tutor and members discuss their own written self-assessment of the presentation. The self-assessment is written after the group has discussed a video recording of their presentation made by their tutor. The tutor evaluates the presentation in discussion with them, negotiates what grade the group will receive for their presentation and guides them on how to make their next presentation more effective.

In a course on society – environment relationships, two student groups debate for and against the proposition that "Animals and plants have a right to existence of themselves; their value is not just a function of their usefulness to humans". Each group has a student advocate who organises it's argument and calls on the other students in the group to present aspects of their case as witnesses. The other students in the class act as jurors with the tutor. They judge the arguments, and which side has presented its arguments more effectively. Each group gets a mark which forms part of its final assessment for that course. Next week the jurors will be acting as advocate or witnesses and their group performance will be similarly assessed.

In an environmental course which spans two terms and incorporates a vacation field course held away from Oxford, the students in their first term, with their tutors' assistance choose an environmental issue to investigate in the field course area. This leads into a project proposal session, in which students justify their project to another student group, who in turn explain it to the staff. Before they get to the field course area groups are responsible for arranging interviews, ensuring that they know how to create and administer questionnaires, use equipment and so on. On the field course, student groups work essentially unsupervised during the day – knowing they have to complete the task in the time available. They also recognise that in the second term they will be assessed as a group on spoken and written presentations of what they have learnt from their investigations.

> Students may need to use skills in a variety of contexts and obtain feedback in a variety of ways.

> The assessment system must incorporate assessment of skills.

37

Rationale

A shared rationale will help staff to develop a coherent approach.

The central reasons for teaching this way are fourfold:

- Most of the staff were dissatisfied with the lecture as a predominant teaching method. They experimented with alternative ways of students' learning Geography and found that methods such as these were far more effective.

- Methods were seen as contributing to the students' developing confidence in themselves.

- It became clear that these methods developed students' employability. This is particularly important as Geography generally does not lead into any clearly defined career.

- Again, though this was not the original stimulus, it became clear that many of these methods enabled students to work far more independently of staff and helped staff to cope with higher student:staff ratios. However, all these methods require careful supervision by staff and some of them require extensive staff time.

Integrating skills development across a degree programme

Elaborate and sophisticated schemes may grow from small-scale experiments.

At first exercises were developed for individual courses. They were experiments which individual staff developed into effective ways of delivering individual courses. This was an important stage for staff to gain confidence in using new methods, including finding out what did not work for them. It also allowed other staff to be convinced by their success and to incorporate them into their own courses, and for external examiners to endorse the alternative assessment methods, such as assessing groups, spoken presentations, which these courses required.

However, there were problems in this piecemeal approach, notably the repetition in different courses of very similar exercises which did not require students to develop their skills to a higher level. Staff also perceived a danger in some students' avoiding courses which focused on particular skills: educationally staff felt all students should be required to develop certain key skills.

There were evident problems in incorporating a progressive development of agreed key skills into a modular framework, which in part allowed student choice of modules, and meant that Geography staff had no control over at least half of a student's programme.

After experimenting with various structures the staff have now decided to:

- identify the key skills they wish to develop;

- create six compulsory modules (three in year one, two in year two and one in year three) through which these skills will be progressively developed;

- offer other modules that focus on particular skills, but allow students to choose the rest of their Geography programme freely.

Problems

Although staff consider that these methods have been highly effective in developing students as geographers and in aiding their employability, there have been problems. These include:

- Student resistance. Initially there was some student resistance, particularly from third-year students used to traditional methods. When the "alternative methods" were introduced from day one of year one these problems largely disappeared. Indeed students became advocates for these methods to staff on their non-Geography courses.

- Assessment. Initially staff were unsure how to assess group work and spoken presentations. Despite practice having been developed and refined this is still an issue of debate.

- Consensus. It can be hard for a group of staff to agree on what are the key skills, how they are best developed and assessed and the balance between a skills-orientated curriculum and academic knowledge. However, like the student groups, they have to create a compromise they feel is satisfactory and that can pass the scrutiny of internal and external validation panels (they are then assessed as a group on their written and spoken presentation!)

A typical exercise is explained below. Many others are set out in detail in Jenkins and Pepper, 1988.

> **Students not used to skills development may be resistant to change.**

> **Developing comprehensive schemes involves careful attention to problems.**

Simulation of Technical Experts Bidding for a Contract

Brief description

Groups of about four students represent different technical groups who are bidding for a contract. Each group espouses a different analytical technique and argues that the contract should be given to them because of the superiority of that technique.

Skills developed

Communicating technical issues to a non-specialist audience; working in groups, speaking and report writing.

Suitable courses

Soil Types and their Management. Particularly suitable for Science and Technology courses.

What the teacher does

Establish the topic to be investigated. This approach is well suited to practical problems where contrasting or conflicting "technical" solutions can be used. For example, one simulation involves an Indian state which, as a basis for an agricultural development programme, requests international assistance in carrying out a soil survey. Students represent different "technical" groups, arguing the value of contrasting methods of soil analysis.

Students are divided into groups, each group being given a particular technical approach to master. The teacher gives guidance over reading and sets out the timetable and what is required.

The teacher then plays the role of the client, inviting bids for a contract of work. This can be done solely by a written statement. Alternatively the teacher can give an aural presentation (perhaps accompanied by a written statement). The "client's" statement or presentation should acquaint students with the practical problem for which a solution is required and should give them all the necessary background information. It is very important that the "client's" needs should not be stated from a technical perspective. Rather it should be from someone in an official position facing a practical problem and requiring specialist advice.

It is very important that the client's needs are stated in a very professional manner for it sets the tone for what follows. That is why you, the teacher, may choose to play the role of the client.

You may choose to see the various groups separately before they do a presentation, helping to clarify their understanding of the technical issues and thinking through how to communicate them in a non-technical way.

The class then takes on the form of competitive technical presentations for a business contract. You as client are in the chair. Each group has to make a presentation in its bid to get the "contract". Your guidelines will have indicated that the presentation must state the basis of the methodology. An effective way of them doing this is through a poster. Each group then has to make a verbal presentation to the client saying why its method should be used to solve the problem. After each group has done a presentation, it is questioned by the client (you) and the competing groups. Here it is important that the questioning is probing and seeks to uncover whether they really understand the technical issues involved and can explain why their approach is the best buy. After all student groups have completed their presentation "the client" says who is to get the contract. You as teacher then state your marks and your reasons.

Problems for the teacher

This technique is probably most suited to classes of 10 – 20 students. As the number in each group should be kept to 2 – 4 and each group has to have a very different perspective it can be difficult to get enough competing methodologies to meet the needs of a large class size. There is a limit to the number of presentations which people can assimilate (even if they are spread over a number of class sessions). Many presentations can take up too much time from the course.

It is essential that there is a good range of accessible published material on each of the perspectives. You will need to spend much time before the exercise making sure all these resources are available.

Students have been set a hard task. The material which each group has to assimilate may well be difficult. Groups also have to be able to communicate it in a non-technical way. Particularly if the (reading) resources are limited or difficult, students can get discouraged. You probably need to see them periodically before the presentation to advise and encourage.

(Devised by Professor Martin Haigh, Oxford Brookes University)

40

6.2 Problem-solving skills in Engineering

At Coventry University the second year of the B.Eng. has a problem-based alternative: Automotive Engineering Design. This course illustrates how a comprehensive approach to skills development involves complete integration into the teaching and learning methods of the course and also into the assessment. The course abandoned a formal lecture programme and teacher-imposed timetable. The syllabus was greatly reduced. Exams were dropped and the assessment tasks could no longer be tackled by regurgitation. The course involves several key features:

Problem-based learning

Students tackle design problems in order to generate a need to find out. The pace at which new problems are introduced depends on the level of students' understanding rather than on a fixed timetable. Lecturing is limited to that required to solve the problem and does not follow a formal schedule. The problems are so structured as to clarify learners' needs and to limit the length of formal teaching to what is required to meet those needs.

Integrating skills development may involve radical new curricula with new learning processes.

Reflection on learning

Students keep a learning journal in which they record their reflections on learning. Tutors respond in writing to students' entries in their journals, making comments designed to encourage further, and deeper, reflection, rather than to correct or assess. Students also maintain a learning log which contains a full record of the content of their learning, particularly the process of learning. Coursework is also structured to provide a period of reflection and to enable generalisations of knowledge to take place. The logs are assessed and marks contribute to the overall assessment of the year.

Where learning processes are complex an integrating focus such as a log may help to avoid fragmentation.

Independent group work

Students spend most of their time in teams throughout most of the year. Students tutor each other and co-operate on problems and projects.

Learning by doing

Students spend most of their time in a purpose-built design studio engaged in engineering design process activities. The studio has clusters of chairs around drawing boards, CAD terminals along one side and an area at one end for impromptu larger group work and lectures. Formal instruction represents a very small proportion of learning time.

Project work

Periodically throughout the year students tackle week-long projects through which they integrate and apply the knowledge and skills they have developed through group problem-based work. Towards the end of the year these projects are carried out on an individual basis.

41

Assessment

The assessment has also been radically changed. Instead of exams the assessment involves the learning logs, group-based tasks and individual project work, some moderated by oral examinations at which students are required to explain their design decisions. The oral assessment process is developed through informal orals used regularly as part of normal classes. The orals have proved problematic.

The following summary of a five-week sequence of sessions on Solid Mechanics illustrates the way problem-based learning works in practice. Learning how to solve problems, work in groups and learn Engineering is completely integrated with Engineering knowledge and skills. Note the explicit use of the experiential learning cycle (see 3.1) and the central place of reflection, or monitoring, in the process (see 4.1).

Process and content are completely integrated here in the way students learn to tackle problems.

Solid Mechanics

Week 1 Day 1   50-minute studio session

The problem: vehicle suspension systems.

Level of students' knowledge: no formal study of suspension system analysis; first-year Engineering Science; assumed awareness of basic car design features. The problem starts with the students' being asked in groups to discuss what the purpose of a suspension system is. The lecturer assists by stimulating discussion and challenging perceptions (35 minutes). In a plenary session each group is asked to contribute their conclusions and the lecturer lists significant student responses (15 minutes).

Week 1 Day 2   100-minute studio session

The study of the suspension system analysis is taken further by asking the students in their groups to discuss how the system works and how they would design it. The lecturer circulates among the groups to stimulate and challenge, but not to answer or tell (70 minutes). In a plenary session the groups attempt to explain how the system works. The lecturer exploits the session to identify the knowledge and skills required to design a suspension system.

Week 2 Day 1   50-minute studio session

Introductory lecture on vector methods (40 minutes). This is followed by a questioning session to identify any problems with the lecture material (10 minutes).

Week 2 Day 2   100-minute studio session

A practical assignment is handed out requiring the students in their groups to build with balsa wood and cotton a three-dimensional vector system. They have to measure parameters of the system and calculate the same parameters using basic trigonometry (O-level Maths) comparing the two results. Finally they are required to reflect on their experience and draw out general rules for future application.

Week 3 Day 1   50-minute studio session

Students are reminded of the experiential learning cycle. In their groups they are requested to continue their reflection started on Day 2 of the previous week, to generalise their new found knowledge and consider its application to the problems of the suspension system, identifying any perceived problems in its application (40 minutes). They are then required to commit this to paper and share it with the group in a plenary session (10 minutes).

Week 3 Day 2   100-minute studio session

This is an interactive lecture session aimed at developing the principles of geometric modelling of three-dimensional systems, with the suspension system as the problem base. The interaction is achieved by posing problems for the groups which they should be able to solve from their observations of physical structures (60 minutes).

A formative assignment is introduced which applies the modelling techniques to a known suspension system and requires the students to build in balsa wood the geometric model created, checking measured dimensions against calculated ones (40 minutes).

Week 4 Days 1 and 2   150-minute studio session

The whole session is given up to the assignment set the previous week. The lecturer assists in a tutorial mode, advising on methods and also on recording learning in the log book. The lecturer's solution is provided at the end of the session against which the students assess themselves.

Week 5 Day 1   50-minute studio session

The whole session involves interaction in which students generalise their experience from the assignment and resolve any difficulties remaining after their self-assessment.

Week 5 Day 2   100-minute studio session

A summative assignment is introduced on the geometric modelling of a different type of suspension. The students are each required to log all their own work, "warts and all", and hand it in on Day 1 of week 7.

Source: Gibbs, G. (1992) *Improving the Quality of Student Learning*. Bristol: Technical and Educational Services, chapter 7, pp. 59-76

Generalising from a specific experience is crucial to transferring skills from one context to another.

6.3 Entrepreneurial skills in Hotel and Catering Management

Hotel and Catering Management lecturers on the degree programme from which the examples below are drawn would probably want to argue that essentially everything they do is "entrepreneurial" in some way, and that the whole list of enterprise skills are needed by the successful entrepreneur. The three examples described here focus explicitly on entrepreneurial skills as well as involving a range of other transferable skills. The emphasis in these examples is on learning activities demanding the use of transferable skills and on assessment methods which emphasise the use of these skills. There is, however, little emphasis on acquiring the necessary skills, and if preceding modules did not contain the necessary training exercises then many students would find the demands excessive.

6.3.1 Planning a catering event

One obvious example of a module with an entrepreneurial focus requires the students, in teams, to design, plan, execute and review a catering event, including its financial management. The type of event is decided upon by the team – a Mexican evening, a wine and cheese evening, or whatever. In order to run the event, extra "staff" have to be recruited by the team from other students on the module and 10% of the assessment is for the production of the group's financial accounts.

The course involves entrepreneurial activities with real financial consequences.

Some groups have been exceptionally entrepreneurial, one gaining sponsorship from Unipart for an evening celebrating Oxford United's promotion to the first division, another running a "special needs" charity fund-raising evening, financing the evening through company donations.

The module attempts to find the right balance between reality and the need to give the students sufficient support. For example, the wine and cheese event was badly conceived and inadequately marketed so was postponed to be "relaunched" later in the term, rather than allowed to proceed and fail commercially.

In addition to their own event, each group also has to act as a team of consultants reviewing one of the other group's events, with this review forming part of the assessment.

Students have to deal with changes to their group membership and review in an essay how they coped.

This module also covers "the management of change", with one member of each original group being moved, before the events, into a different group. Another part of the assessment includes an essay reviewing the performance of the team, including consideration of how it coped with this personnel change. Overall the various assessments involve the students in using presentation skills (twice), producing two written reports, one on the work of another group, and presenting a set of financial accounts; all this work is assessed as a group product. Group work marks are distributed by the team. Individually students write an essay. Their performance in the catering event itself, and the preparatory laboratory programme before it, are also assessed individually, but only contribute 10% of the marks.

6.3.2 Hotel case study

In a final-year module, intended to bring many aspects of the course together, groups perform as a team of consultants retained by a leisure group to carry out a study on a recently acquired hotel.

They are presented with the following remit:

The Managing Director of GBC Leisure requires you to submit a report which:

(a) analyses and evaluates the information provided, including the financial statement, in order to identify the main problems currently facing the hotel;

(b) within the constraints of the existing information, produces an outline marketing plan for the hotel (covering the next two years);

(c) outlines your operational proposals necessary to make the hotel as profitable as possible during this period.

They are provided with financial statements for the last two years, a year-old market research report and other relevant data.

In the past this has been pretty much a paper exercise, but the module is being modified so that the groups will start by visiting a particular town to examine the tourism, hotels and other leisure and hospitality businesses. Each group will then be allocated to a specific hotel or hospitality operation and be expected to analyse its operation, finance and marketing, leading to a comprehensive report as before.

6.3.3 Corporate Management module

In this module, as a major part of the coursework, students in groups have the choice of entering one of two national competitions. They may either produce a marketing award proposal for entry in the National Catering Business Game computer simulation, competing against other universities, or develop a £25,000 marketing plan for the London Tourist Board to compete for the London Tourist Board's Presidents' Marketing Awards.

This work counts for 30% of the assessment. The best three entries are actually entered in the competitions. Some students have, in fact, criticised aspects of the computer simulation as insufficiently realistic and may attempt to develop their own as an independent study module.

Other assessments in the module include an individual response to a case study, an individually produced training package which can be applied within a small group, an individually constructed annotated bibliography, and an organisation study which is partially assessed through a presentation.

Student groups study business and write reports proposing changes.

Student groups enter national marketing competitions.

Monitoring transferable skills

Without monitoring, skills may not improve. Monitoring involves feedback and reflection on one's own performance. This section provides guidelines on how to give and receive feedback and some examples and checklists which involve monitoring.

7.1 Giving and receiving feedback

An essential part of the process of learning enterprise skills is receiving feedback on our performance. The problem is that we often defend ourselves against the possibility of negative feedback and so fail to listen and thus to act upon what may be very helpful information. On the other hand much feedback tends to be presented in such a way that it creates a defensive reaction. The following guidelines embody two basic principles: the existential one of "I can speak of my own experience; I cannot speak of yours," and the learning one: "I have heard what you say and this is what I propose to do."

Giving feedback

- Invite the recipient to speak first. This fosters the skills of self-criticism and protects self-respect.

- Be specific rather than general. To be told that one is disorganised will probably not be as useful as to be told: "When you lost your place during the lecture and couldn't find the right notes I found it distracting."

- Balance positive and negative feedback. Positive feedback on its own allows no room for improvement and negative feedback on its own is discouraging.

- Direct your feedback towards behaviour that your fellow student can control. It would not be helpful, for example, to comment on someone's lisp.

- Ask for confirmation from a third party. For example, if you are giving feedback to your fellow student at the end of a seminar then check out the accuracy of your feedback with them.

Receiving feedback

- Listen to the feedback without comment. You will hear more if you concentrate on listening rather than explaining or justifying yourself.

- Ask for clarification at the end. You need to be sure that you understand exactly what your fellow student is saying about you and what evidence the comments are based on.

- Devise action plans. Specify ways in which you want to change, new ideas you want to try, etc.

- If there is anything your fellow students can do or not do to help you achieve your action plans, tell them.

- Keep a written record. This can be used for later reflection, action planning and appraisal interviews.

- Thank your fellow student for their feedback.

Following these guidelines on giving and receiving feedback can make the process easier and more effective.

47

It can be useful to run an exercise with students in which, in threes, they take turns for one to give feedback to a second on some aspect of their behaviour (such as their involvement in a seminar group) with the third observing, using the above checklist to notice and comment on how feedback was given and received.

7.2 Monitoring project work in teams

Students are often asked to work in teams for quite long periods without outside support. They are bound to run into all kinds of difficulties, but social conventions may make it very difficult to raise issues which might imply criticism of individuals or of the team as a whole. It is often necessary to use an exercise explicitly designed to make public what team members know or suspect but which they are not acting on.

There are many checklists of the kind offered below which focus on different aspects of team behaviour: leadership, goal setting and task orientation, emotional tone, co-operation, meeting skills and so on. This list identifies the problems that teams are most likely to encounter and invites group members to say whether or not they are occurring in their team. In effect it gives permission to team members to speak up.

Review checklists can be used in a variety of ways to monitor skills.

Such checklists can be used in a variety of ways:

- The whole team can go through the checklist together, discussing what they think is happening in the team. This runs the risk of members' not speaking up and the team colluding in pretending that nothing is going wrong.

- Individuals within a team can fill in the checklist alone and then pool and discuss their responses and ideas on what they might do to rectify the situation. This may still confront individuals with difficulties if the team appears to have responded to the checklist differently from themselves.

- Students can form cross-over groups made up of one member from each team, and discuss the checklist in relation to their own team. This is much more likely to lead to open and honest discussion of problems. Students can then go back to their own teams with some confidence and some ideas about what to do to tackle problems.

It can be helpful for teams to be explicit about the problems they have identified and to record decisions about what to do to tackle problems. A future review could then check on the extent to which these actions have solved the identified problems. Teams need to monitor their own performance on a fairly regular basis – for example, having five minutes of review at the end of each meeting. Even a short time spent on process can pay off handsomely in productivity and learning outcomes.

A simple exercise to monitor team work might take the following form, with all teams together in one room:

Project Teams Review

Stage 1

Form cross-over groups made up of one member of each of the teams.

This is helpful to widen the range of experience being reviewed and also to give students the freedom to discuss their own team unchallenged.

Stage 2

Each student in the cross-over groups, in turn, reports:

"One thing we have done as a team which has helped us to work effectively and learn is . . ."

Followed by an open discussion.

Stage 3

Each person in turn reports:

"One thing which goes wrong/which we have trouble with in our team is . . ."

and seeks help from the others in suggesting ways to tackle and overcome the problem.

Stage 4

The teams re-form and discuss what they think they can do to build on their successes and overcome their problems in the future.

Stage 5

Each team reports to the whole class one change they will make:

"One thing we are going to do differently in the way we work is . . ."

Structuring reviews can help students to consider issues and their implications more thoroughly.

The following checklist may help students to identify the problems that their team is facing:

Teamwork Checklist: What is going wrong?		
Tick	**What might be going wrong**	**Comments**
☐	Not clarifying what your task or objective is	
☐	Not checking on progress	
☐	Not checking on the time	
☐	Not clarifying or recording what has been decided	
☐	Not clarifying who is going to do what	
☐	Not clarifying what has to be done by when	
☐	Not establishing procedures for handling meetings	
☐	Not keeping to agreed procedures	
☐	Not listening to each other	
☐	Allowing individuals to dominate and others to withdraw	
☐	Not compromising individuals' wants for the sake of the team	
☐	Not recognising the feelings of members of the team	
☐	Not contributing equally to the progress of the team	

Source: Gibbs, G. (1994) *Learning in Teams: A Student Manual.* Oxford Centre for Staff Development.

Students should complete this checklist independently before discussing it in their team.

7.3   Monitoring seminar presentations

Giving seminar presentations is probably the most common form of communication skills exercise in many courses. Using the ideas outlined here can help to ensure that students actually learn some skills from all the practice they get.

Students can be helped in a variety of ways to monitor how they are developing their skills at giving effective seminar presentations.

Review exercises

In the early stages of a course, teachers can run exercises similar to the one set out in section 5.3.1 which require students to identify what they have learnt about seminar presentations in previous courses and what they now need work on. These exercises can also help students to define with you appropriate criteria for assessment or to internalise your criteria.

Students can be involved in defining the criteria used to monitor skills.

Guidelines

Written guidelines, developed by you, from published sources, or by students in previous years, can make clear what is expected and what students should do when preparing for a seminar. Here a tutor says what not to do, when giving a group presentation.

Common faults

- The speaker painstakingly reads from a script, seldom looking at the audience. It is forbidden to read a script. You may, however, speak to the audience from notes which set out the main points of your argument.

- "The centre does not hold." It has been at times difficult to see the central question being considered. In making a report, people should generally consider a limited number of themes and make sure the report emphasises these.

- At times some presentations overwhelm people with a mass of detail. Detail is important but you must limit it to what is essential and show how it relates to your general themes.

- The reports and answers to subsequent questions are dominated by one person. In no way is it a group performance. A basic rule is that all have to be equally involved in the whole presentation, including answering questions.

Descriptions of how to be ineffective can help students to spot their mistakes.

Checklists

Checklists of points to consider when giving a presentation can be used by students to consider how their planned presentation can be improved.

Assessment criteria

Make clear the criteria by which the presentation will be assessed. If students know and understand the criteria from the beginning of the course, most will use these to guide their own performance.

Self- and peer-assessment

Requiring self-assessment forms to be completed after a presentation, can result in students' reflecting deeply on this experience and starting to plan their next presentation. Requiring students to watch a videotape (or listen to a sound tape) of their seminar, and asking them to comment on this as part of a self-assessment, can considerably affect their self-awareness.

Seeing yourself on video can have a powerful effect.

Seminar Video Review

Having seen the video recording of your presentation:

- What were its strengths?

- What were its weaknesses?

- Looking ahead to your next presentation, reflecting on the one you have just done, what do you now intend to do differently?

Seminar presentations lend themselves to both self- and peer-assessment. Peer-assessment can aid those assessing to consider how their presentation will meet these criteria. (Carefully selecting the first presentation to ensure it is a strong one can lead many other students to rethink what they are going to do. You probably won't need to say a thing.)

Time out

Review can help students to identify common strengths and weaknesses in different presentations.

After a small number of students have done their presentations it can help them and those following to take "time out" in class to review the presentations so far. What have been the strengths of these presentations? What have been the weaknesses? What should those who still have to present pay special attention to?

Tutorials

Requiring all those presenting to see you for a brief tutorial before they make their presentations can affect how they prepare. Obviously, given the number of students you have to deal with you have to ration this time carefully. But the requirement to attend a ten-minute tutorial and to bring a written outline of their proposed presentation and two issues they want to discuss with you can dramatically change their presentation.

Course design

Students need to see self- and peer-assessment as not one-off experiences but as part of their overall development. Subject groups who design student programmes to ensure that presentation skills introduced in year one are reflected on and developed in years two and three will encourage students to periodically review their progress.

Portfolios and profiles

Mechanisms such as portfolios which require students to put together and comment upon a number of seminar presentations, and profiles (see Section 10) can enable students to see how they have progressed and what they still need to work on.

52

This form can be used either by the tutor or by students in a seminar group to give feedback to the seminar presenters:

Seminar Presentation Feedback Form

1 Pace	too fast		about right		too slow
	☐	☐	☐	☐	☐

2 Quantity of material	too much		about right		too little
	☐	☐	☐	☐	☐

3 Clarity and structure	very clear		adequate		muddled
	☐	☐	☐	☐	☐

4 Interest	very interesting		adequate		dull
	☐	☐	☐	☐	☐

5 Notes and handouts	full and clear		adequate	poor	none
	☐	☐	☐	☐	☐

6 Use of visual aids	very helpful		adequate	poor	none
	☐	☐	☐	☐	☐

7 Discussion	very engaging		adequate	poor	none
	☐	☐	☐	☐	☐

8 References	full and clear		adequate	poor	none
	☐	☐	☐	☐	☐

Best features of the seminar:

Suggestions for improvement for your next seminar presentation:

Feedback forms help to structure feedback and separate out different components of a skill.

53

Assessing transferable skills

It is not enough that the products of the use of transferable skills, such as written reports, are assessed. It is necessary to reward and comment upon the use of skills in preparing the product. The examples here focus on the most common examples of the assessment of product at the expense of process: group work and written work.

8.1   Assessing teamwork

It is possible to observe students while they are working in teams, using one of a range of checklists. However, it is difficult not to change the behaviour of a group you are observing, and the meeting you sample may be very different from other meetings at different stages in the team's life. It is also time-consuming to observe students while they are working in teams. Assessment is likely to have to rely on students' self-reporting and on their awareness and understanding of group processes.

Students should be asked to answer the following questions:

- What steps have you taken to organise your teamwork?

- What steps have you taken to monitor the effectiveness of your team?

- What steps have you taken to improve the effectiveness of your team?

- What problems have you encountered in working as a team and how did you tackle them?

- If you were able to embark on a second, similar task as a team, what would be different about the way you went about working as a team, and why?

The criteria to be used in assessing this report could be:

- the range and appropriateness of organisational steps and strategies adopted;

- the range and usefulness of methods used to monitor effectiveness, and quality of evidence obtained;

- the range and effectiveness of steps taken to improve team performance;

- the perceptiveness with which team problems were identified and diagnosed;

- the range, appropriateness and effectiveness of steps taken to overcome problems;

- the quality of review and action planning for a second team task.

For formal assessment purposes you can use a variety of devices which focus on process:

- Ask teams to submit a "team process report" on completion of their work.

- Require such a report as one section of a team project report.

- Require individuals to submit their own individual team process reports.

Students will need clues about what aspects of their teamwork to write about.

55

- Hold short vivas with either whole teams or individual members of teams, asking questions about the team's operation.

- Use an exam question of the form: "Give an account of the way your team strove to operate effectively. What general issues emerged about the operation of teams? What steps might you personally take to address these issues next time you work in a team?" You can even warn students in advance that they will get such an exam question – the only way they can "revise" for it is to reflect on the operation of their team and find out more about explanations and alternatives!

8.2 Assessing the skill components of essay and report writing

Presumably the skills used in writing essays and reports are assessed every time a tutor puts a grade on such a piece of coursework, but the danger is that all too often such assessment is subjective and implicit, and offers no formative help to the student. To overcome this there are three golden rules.

1 Specify the skills: If you make clear exactly what skills you are expecting, the student does not have to guess what they are – and risk the chance of guessing wrongly. It will also help you when you come to mark the piece of work as the skills specification can act as a checklist. And you can check your subjective reaction against this set of criteria. It can then help you to give feedback to the student, enabling you to identify in which of the skills they are weak or strong, and forming a useful starting point for any dialogue with the student in a subsequent tutorial.

2 Model the skills: In addition to stating the expected skills, it can help to model them by indicating, through examples, what good and bad practice in each skill might look like. This can include providing sample reports from previous years, for example.

3 Allocate marks: Unless all the required skills are equally important, which seems unlikely, weighting them with different shares of the overall mark will clearly indicate to students those which are most valued and which they need to spend most time on.

If these three rules are kept when the assignment is set, you can expect an overall increase in the quality of work that is done, with the beneficial spin-off that you may need to spend less time on remedial feedback. If the skills are included as part of an assignment attachment sheet (see the example that follows), listing all the criteria for the assignment, this can also reduce the amount of time needing to be spent on writing comments.

Such sheets can also be used in the development of self- and peer-assessment in that the student can be asked to fill out the form for their own work (or for a peer's) before you mark it, and then any discrepancies between their mark and yours can be discussed. It is possible to build up students' assessment skills until their marking decisions can be allowed to stand.

The assessment of skills is often submerged by the assessment of content.

Students need to see where marks have come from.

56

Assignment Attachment Sheet

Knowledge

Text	deep, thorough, detailed	☐	☐	☐	☐	☐	superficial
Author	wide knowledge used in analysis	☐	☐	☐	☐	☐	no knowledge or not used
Genre	wide knowledge used in analysis	☐	☐	☐	☐	☐	no knowledge or not used
Historical and social context	wide knowledge used in analysis	☐	☐	☐	☐	☐	no knowledge or not used

Essay

Structure	clear, logical structure	☐	☐	☐	☐	☐	confused
Quotations	correct, purposeful use, properly referenced	☐	☐	☐	☐	☐	incorrect, arbitrary use
Other sources	wide range, relevant properly referenced	☐	☐	☐	☐	☐	few, irrelevant not properly referenced
Grammar, spelling	correct	☐	☐	☐	☐	☐	many errors

Personal

Response to text	vivid, personal	☐	☐	☐	☐	☐	little response
Viewpoint	clearly expressed	☐	☐	☐	☐	☐	no viewpoint
Creativity	imaginative, surprising	☐	☐	☐	☐	☐	predictable

Critical theory

Understanding	clear grasp	☐	☐	☐	☐	☐	little grasp
Use of methods	wide range	☐	☐	☐	☐	☐	little or inappropriate

Comments:

Grade this essay deserves with reasons:

8.3 Self- and peer-assessment of written assignments

All marking of written work involves the use of criteria and standards, many of which are never made explicit and, even when they are, rarely get internalised by the students. Frequently there is a semi-conscious hit-or-miss approach in which the students gradually learn to conform to the requirements. But ask them to spell out what these are and they'd be hard pressed to come up with an answer. The main reason for this lacuna seems to be the external imposition of criteria and standards and the lack of shared discussion with other students on what seems to count in getting good marks.

If, however, students can be engaged in the process of deciding criteria, negotiating standards and applying both of these in marking and giving feedback for written assignments, they can not only learn a professional skill – that of making judgements about the value of their own and others' work – but can relieve the tutor of a lot of tedious and repetitive work in giving detailed feedback on each assignment.

Involving students in all aspects of assessment can support the learning of skills.

Stage 1 Generating criteria (30 minutes)

When setting an assignment put students into groups of four to six and ask them to share what they think will count for a competent piece of work by completing sentences such as:

"It will look good if I . . ."

"I'll feel OK about it if . . ."

"I know I get good marks when I . . ."

Ask each group in turn to shout out one of their criteria and write them up on the board or OHP. Invite them to consider these when writing the assignment.

Make it clear to them at this stage that you expect the assignments to be handed in at the start of a future class and that they will be looked at by the same groups before being passed on to you.

Stage 2 Students undertake the assignment

Stage 3 Peer marking (30 minutes)

At the class in question, ask students, working in the same groups as before, to pass their completed assignments round so that each member of the group reads everyone else's. Ask them then to write on a sheet of paper an agreed "provisional grade" for each piece of work with a brief comment to justify it. Collect the work in for marking.

When you mark the work, there are two options:

- write comments on the script but keep your marks or grades hidden;

- write your comments on a separate sheet of paper, but again keep the marks hidden.

58

Stage 4 Detailed feedback between pairs (20 minutes)

Before you hand the work back, organise the scripts so as to pair students gaining better grades with those gaining poor ones, as far as you can, and thereafter on a random basis. Tell them that you want them to work in pairs and that you are going to hand the scripts back to the opposite partner such that A sees B's script and B sees A's. The task then is for A to mark B's and vice versa. Depending on how you proceeded in Stage 3, ask each surrogate tutor either to decide what grade to give to their partner's work on the basis of your comments or to write both comments and marks first before you give them access to your comments at a later stage. Once each surrogate tutor has decided the comments and grades, ask them to get together with their partner and give them a ten-minute tutorial, i.e. ten minutes each way. Do not reveal your grade at this stage.

Stage 5 (10 – 20 minutes)

Ask whether anyone in the class minds if there is public discussion of their grades. If not, invite each surrogate tutor in turn to call out the grade they gave for their partner's work. Then reveal your grade for the same work; where there is a big discrepancy ask their reasons and give yours. At this stage you may decide to accept the surrogate tutor's mark, negotiate a new mark or agree to differ, with the promise of a second and final opinion from another tutor. If anyone does object to this public discussion then you can go through the same process with her or his surrogate tutor privately in the class.

Stage 6 (30 minutes)

Now ask the pairs to write a shared list of "what makes a good written assignment" (or whatever you call the piece of work) for five minutes. Then ask pairs to join others to form fours and to produce a composite list of the most important criteria (ten minutes).

Finally ask for one criterion from each four in turn and write them up on the board. Process these through open discussion into a shortlist of not fewer than five and not more than ten criteria. You may have to add one or two of your own but that is unlikely. Explain that you will expect these criteria, weighted appropriately, to apply to subsequent assignments and that students will be expected to assess their own work using them and to write a justification that will itself receive a mark.

Then, next time you collect a written assignment for marking each student will have thought more carefully about how their own piece of work measures up to the criteria. Furthermore, you will have some pointers from the self-assessments as to which scripts are going to need more attention than others and some measure of students' ability to assess their own competence.

Profiling

9.1 Types of profiling

Profiles are summaries of learning outcomes and are often used as a way of indicating the range and quality of the skills students have acquired. There is a wide range of types of profile used for different purposes.

Assessment of course outcomes

Some courses, such as new Certificate in Management courses based on the Management Charter Initiative set of management competences, summarise what students have learnt' using a profile of the competences which have been acquired. These profiles are used at the outset to help students to set targets and to negotiate learning tasks, and at the end as a record of achievement on the course. Such uses are likely to increase as the National Vocational Qualification movement expands into higher education.

Assessment of transferable skills

On many courses, while the course content is assessed in conventional ways and leads to a single grade, mark or classification, the transferable skills developed are assessed qualitatively and expressed on a profile, which describes the level reached but is not associated with marks. Such profiles are often in the form of lists of skills and accompanying sets of rating scales.

Records of achievement

Sometimes a profile is a collection of evidence about what has been undertaken and achieved. It may take the form of a folder containing a range of documents collected as a student went through their course: a letter from an employer, a form assessing a group project presentation, a reference, a list of skills involved in a major project, and so on. Such profiles may be collected by the students themselves and may not even be validated or checked by a tutor. They may include skill profiles, either self-assessed or self- and tutor-assessed.

Assessment of prior learning (APL)

APL can produce a profile of past qualifications, experiences or competences. It may be linked to the assessment of course outcomes and in effect exempt the student from having to take parts of a course.

Records of work-based learning

It is becoming increasingly common to use profiles to frame and direct work-based learning – to set objectives, to negotiate with work-based supervisors, and to aid in the assessment of the outcomes of work-based learning. Such profiles may include lists of experiences and evidence of learning outcomes in relation to learning contracts. They may include skill profiles or lists of competences.

> Profiling is used for a variety of purposes, not all of which are concerned with transferable skills.

Personal development and career orientation

Profiles are also used as self-development exercises whether or not they are linked to assessment or course goals. Such profiling may involve personal skills reviews, personal objective setting, action planning, career planning and development exercises.

9.2   Sample profiles (CNAA, 1992)

9.2.1 A Certificate of Education profile

This example is an extract from a prescribed learning outcome profiling system used by the Certificate of Education (FE) course at the University of Central Lancashire at Preston. Students must show that they are competent in all 56 elements of competence in order to be awarded the Certificate of Education. There are no grades and the award is made on a pass/fail basis. The whole course (i.e. the teaching, learning and assessment process) is structured around the prescribed competences.

Document 1 Portfolio of Professional Achievement: Accreditation of competences

Management of learning

Description: The competences listed in this unit are concerned with the delivery of teaching and the promotion of learning through various strategies involving the use of effective teaching methods and the creation of an appropriate environment. These competences will be considered in all of the modules but in particular in modules 1,2,3,4 and 9.

End Competence: The course member is able to create and maintain an optimum learning environment and is able to select and use appropriate methods of teaching. This achievement signifies that the course member has:

No.	Level	Elements of Competence	Evidence Presented	Date	Accreditor's signature
4a	1	Identified the main factors affecting the creation and maintenance of an optimal teaching and learning environment			
4b	1	Discriminated between three basic strategies of teaching and learning (i.e. presentation, interaction and search) in selecting a particular strategy			
4c	1	Delivered learning through a selected variety of methods			
4d	11	Evaluated the implementation of learning strategies for a particular course			
4e	11	Established proficiency in a range of teaching methods but remained responsive to new approaches and innovations			

Document 2 Record of Accreditation Process

Date of discussion	Competence Number	Agreed Form of Evidence	Anticipated Date of Accreditation	Date of Next Meeting	Initials	
					ACC	MEM

9.2.2 A Technical Communications profile

This example is based on the system used by the BA Technical Communications course at Coventry to assess and record the students' learning on the work-based component of the course. The profile records both prescribed and negotiated objectives. The prescribed learning objectives are those which the course team want all students to achieve while on placement, and the negotiated ones are identified and described by the students and workplace assessors at the beginning of the placement and will vary from student to student. These negotiated objectives are agreed with the visiting tutor. The system is also an example of a graded profile. Each learning objective is graded according to a set of performance standards. The total marks accrued from this assessment make up a percentage of the overall degree award.

Profiles may include scales to help students to judge the level of development of skills.

Form 2 Performance Appraisal

Skills	Unsatisfactory (0.0–1.9)	Fair (2.0–2.4)	Good (2.5–2.9)	Very Good (3.0–3.4)	Outstanding (3.5–5.0)
Social Skills Working effectively with others, individually and/ or as a member of a team.	Has not worked effectively with others.	Has some difficulty in working with others, needs to improve.	Has worked effectively with others in straight forward situations.	Has worked very effectively even in difficult situations.	Has demonstrated excellent personal skills, in a wide variety of situations.
Working to Plans Using time, people and other resources effectively to deliver work on time.	Has wasted time, or has not used available resources, or has refused help.	Has attempted to meet deadlines, but needs to make better use of time and/or resources.	Has met deadlines, where these deadlines were not exceptionally demanding.	Has consistently met deadlines, even where this involved extra effort or replanning.	Has planned own work, obtained resources, and met deadlines in demanding situations.
Quality of Work Producing work that is well written/well designed, and is fit for the required purpose.	Has been badly written, numerous errors have been made, had to be redone.	Work has needed extensive correction, shows only basic grasp of principles.	Work has been well written, only needing a modest amount of correction.	Work has been very well written, showing creativity and good design.	Exceptionally high quality, showing creative and innovative flair, always accurate.
Understanding Grasping complex concepts, recognising and solving problems.	Slow on the up-take; has not recognised problems: inadequate technical grasp.	Takes longer than usual to grasp new concepts; does not readily offer solutions to problems.	Generally quick on the up-take; can analyse problems and contribute to solutions.	Grasps new information well; analyses problems well and makes good suggestions.	Has readily grasped complex concepts; perceptive analysis of complex problems.
Learning Accepting criticism, reflecting on their own performance, using this information to raise their level of performance.	Refuses to take criticism; unable to improve level of performance.	Needs prompting to reflect on experiences; makes only fair use of criticism.	Able to reflect on what has been learnt; and change behaviour accordingly.	Actively seeking learning experiences; can improve performance from feedback.	Exceptionally high ability for self reflection; excellent use of feedback.

Overall Comments

Developing Students' Transferable Skills

Bibliography

Adams, J. L. (1987) *Conceptual Blockbusting*. Penguin

Clanchy, J. and Ballard, B. (1981) *Essay Writing for Students*. Longman, Cheshire

CNAA (1992) *Profiling in Higher Education*

Flower, L. (1985) *Problem Solving Strategies for Writing*. Harcourt, Brace, Jovanovich

Gibbs, G. (1994) *Learning in Teams: A Student Guide; Learning in Teams: A Student Manual; Learning in Teams: A Tutor Manual*. Oxford Centre for Staff Development.

Gurdham, M. (1990) *Interpersonal Skills at Work*. Prentice Hall

Habeshaw, S. and Steeds, D. (1998) *53 Communication Exercises for Science Students*. Technical and Educational Services

Habeshaw, T., Habeshaw, S. and Gibbs, G. (1987) *53 Interesting Ways To Help Your Student To Study*. Technical and Educational Services

Jenkins, A. and Pepper, D. M. (1988) *Enhancing Employability and Educational Experiences: A Manual on Teaching Communication and Group Work Skills in Higher Education*. University of Central England, SEDA, Paper 27.

Pegg, M. (1989) *Positive Leadership*. Lifeskills

Richards, J. (1989) *Time Management: A Tutor's Manual*. British Association of Commercial and Industrial Education

Seiwert, L. J. (1989) *Managing your Time*. Kogan Page

Stevens, M. (1987) *Improving your Presentation Skills*. Kogan Page

Storey, R. (1989) *Team Building: A Manual for Trainers*. British Association of Commercial and Industrial Education

Tropman, J. E. (1980) *Effective Meetings*. Sage

Turner, C. (1983) *Developing Interpersonal Skills*. Further Education Staff College

Other publications available from the Oxford Centre for Staff Development

TEACHING MORE STUDENTS

1 Problems and Course Design Strategies
2 Lecturing to More Students
3 Discussion with More Students
4 Assessing More Students
5 Independent Learning with More Students

Video: Teaching More Students

COURSE DESIGN FOR RESOURCE BASED LEARNING

Course Design for Resource Based Learning in Social Science
Course Design for Resource Based Learning in Education
Course Design for Resource Based Learning in Technology
Course Design for Resource Based Learning in Accountancy
Course Design for Resource Based Learning in Built Environment
Course Design for Resource Based Learning in Art & Design
Course Design for Resource Based Learning in Business
Course Design for Resource Based Learning in Humanities
Course Design for Resource Based Learning in Science

LEARNING IN TEAMS

Learning in Teams: A Student Guide
Learning in Teams: A Student Manual
Learning in Teams: A Tutor Manual (in print 1995)

DEVELOPING STUDENTS' TRANSFERABLE SKILLS

STRATEGIES FOR DIVERSIFYING ASSESSMENT

BEING AN EFFECTIVE ACADEMIC

IMPROVING STUDENT LEARNING PROCEEDINGS

DEVELOPING STUDENTS' WRITING